A TRUE BOOK™

Thunderstorms

CHANA STIEFEL

Children's Press®
An Imprint of Scholastic Inc.
New York   Toronto   London   Auckland   Sydney
Mexico City   New Delhi   Hong Kong
Danbury, Connecticut

Content Consultant

K. Shafer Smith, Ph.D.
Associate Professor, Center for Atmosphere Ocean Science
Courant Institute of Mathematical Sciences
New York University
New York, NY

Library of Congress Cataloging-in-Publication Data

Stiefel, Chana, 1968-
  Thunderstorms / by Chana Stiefel.
    p. cm. -- (A true book)
  Includes index.
     ISBN-13: 978-0-531-16884-4 (lib. bdg.)
            978-0-531-21352-0 (pbk.)
     ISBN-10: 0-531-16884-0 (lib. bdg.)
            0-531-21352-8 (pbk.)

1. Thunderstorms--Juvenile literature. I. Title. II. Series.

QC968.2.S85 2009
551.55'4--dc22   2008014790

Produced by Weldon Owen Education Inc.

1 2 3 4 5 6 7 8 9 10 R 18 17 16 15 14 13 12 11 10 09

Find the Truth!

Everything you are about to read is true *except* for one of the sentences on this page.

Which one is **TRUE**?

T or F Lightning never strikes the same place twice.

T or F Weather data are gathered from more than 10,000 stations around the world.

Find the answers in this book

Contents

Sunlight cannot pass through rain clouds because they are full of water or ice particles.

Some studies have shown that elephants will move toward distant thunderstorms to get water.

CHAPTER 1

Storm Brewing

About 2,000 thunderstorms are sweeping across the globe while you read this book. Thunderstorms are rainstorms with lightning and thunder. They can strike almost anywhere, on land or at sea. However, the area around the **equator** produces the most thunderstorms. This region is called the **tropics**. The tropics have plenty of warm, humid air. This is the main ingredient for brewing a thunderstorm.

Tropical Africa is the lightning capital of the world.

The Making of a Thunderstorm

The warmth of the sun causes water to **evaporate** to form water vapor. Warm, damp air rises. As it does, water vapor cools and **condenses** to form clouds. If a lot of damp air rises rapidly, the cloud may form a flat-topped **cumulonimbus cloud**.

Cumulonimbus clouds are thunderstorm "factories." Inside them, water droplets combine to form larger drops. Soon the drops become too heavy to float on the air. They fall as rain or hail.

Cumulonimbus clouds can stretch for miles.

Myths

Ancient cultures came up with their own explanations for the formation of lightning and thunder. The Vikings believed that lightning struck when Thor, the god of weather, threw down his great hammer. Thunder rumbled when his chariot collided with storm clouds. Early Greeks thought that Zeus, the king of gods, threw thunderbolts when he got angry. Several Native American peoples believed that lightning flashed when the mighty god Thunderbird flapped its wings. Peoples of the Pacific Northwest depicted Thunderbird on totem poles.

Flashy and Loud

A bolt of lightning is a huge electrical current. Electrical currents flow when positive electrical charges (+) and negative electrical charges (−) are drawn toward each other.

During an electrical storm, clouds, air, and objects on the ground all become charged with electricity. The top of a storm cloud often acquires a positive charge. The bottom often becomes negatively charged. This causes particles in the surrounding air to become charged as well. Charged particles make excellent **conductors** of electricity between the sky and Earth. Objects on the ground then acquire a positive charge. The stage is set for a cloud-to-ground lightning strike.

When the difference between the positive charges on the ground and the negative charges in a cloud grows strong enough, lightning strikes! An electrical current flows through the charged air.

Lightning travels inside clouds, between clouds, and from clouds to the ground. Cloud-to-cloud lightning is the most common type. The most dangerous kind of lightning is cloud-to-ground.

Types of Lightning

Inside a cloud

Cloud-to-cloud

Cloud-to-ground

Teaming Up

Lightning and thunder are a team. Lightning causes thunder. Thunder is the explosion that you hear when air is suddenly heated by lightning. The air can reach 50,000 °F (27,700 °C). That's more than five times hotter than the sun's surface! This extreme heat causes **molecules** in the air to expand rapidly and vibrate. The vibrations create the boom of thunder.

Each year, lightning strikes Earth about 20 million times.

Forked lightning gets its name from the way the bolt forks on its way down to the ground.

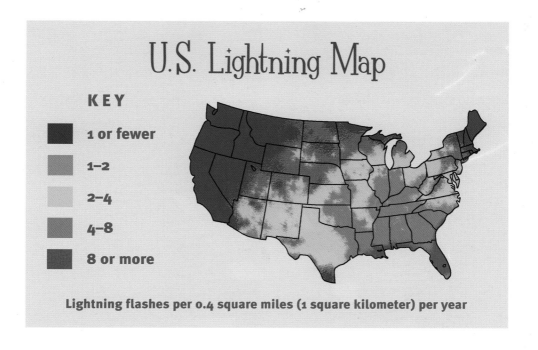

U.S. Lightning Map

KEY

- 1 or fewer
- 1–2
- 2–4
- 4–8
- 8 or more

Lightning flashes per 0.4 square miles (1 square kilometer) per year

Lightning and thunder occur at almost exactly the same time. Yet you see a flash of lightning before you hear the crack of thunder. Light travels nearly a million times faster than sound. The sound of thunder travels one mile (1.6 kilometers) in five seconds. The next time you see a lightning flash, count the seconds until you hear thunder. Divide that number by five. That's how many miles you are away from the thunderstorm.

Lightning Rod

A lightning rod can protect a structure from being damaged by lightning. It is made of a metal that is a good conductor. It carries the strong electrical current from a lightning strike safely to the ground. If the lightning were to strike a material that is not a good conductor, it would do a great deal of heat damage. Lightning usually strikes the highest point. A lightning rod is built to be higher than the structure it is protecting.

How It Works

A simple lightning rod usually consists of three parts. A metal rod is installed on top of a building. Another metal rod is buried in the ground near the building. A thick wire connects the two. The wire carries the electrical charge safely to the ground.

Where It Works

The Empire State Building was designed to serve as a lightning rod for the surrounding area. It is not true that lightning never strikes the same place twice. The Empire State Building is struck by lightning about 100 times a year!

The peak of a cumulonimbus cloud can easily reach 39,000 feet (12,000 meters) or higher.

CHAPTER 2

Zap! Flash! Boom!

The average thunderstorm stretches for 15 miles (24 kilometers) and lasts about 30 minutes. However, more severe storms can span hundreds of miles and whip around for hours. These storms are dramatic, and can be destructive.

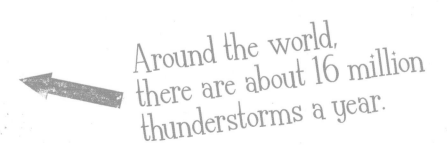

Around the world, there are about 16 million thunderstorms a year.

Severe Thunderstorms

Some thunderstorms are categorized as severe. This means that they produce **tornadoes**, winds higher than 58 miles (93 kilometers) per hour, or large hailstones. Severe thunderstorms can do serious damage. The United States experiences about 100,000 thunderstorms every year. About one in ten of these is classified as severe.

Hailstones are compact balls of ice. They can sometimes be bigger than a grapefruit! They may shred crops and batter cars, windows, and roofs. Hail does about $1,000,000,000 worth of damage a year in the United States.

Large hailstones can fall at speeds of about 100 miles (160 kilometers) per hour.

A severe hailstorm hit Bogotá, Colombia, on November 3, 2007. Firefighters had to dig cars out of the ice. They rescued more than 100 people.

Tornadoes

Under the right conditions, a severe thunderstorm can lead to a tornado. A tornado is a column of high-speed, upward-swirling wind. It extends from the ground to the bottom of a storm cloud. The dramatic shape and dark color of a tornado are direct results of how it is formed.

There are about 1,200 tornadoes in the United States every year. One region of the United States has more tornadoes than anywhere else. Nicknamed Tornado Alley, it has about 300 tornadoes each year.

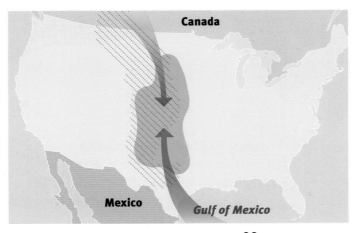

In Tornado Alley, cold, dry air from Canada collides with warm, moist air from the Gulf of Mexico over the Great Plains.

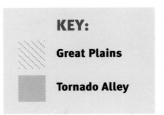

KEY:

Great Plains

Tornado Alley

The Making of a Tornado

1. **Conditions that cause thunderstorms can also lead to tornadoes. First, warm winds close to the ground meet cold winds higher up. The warm air rises.**

2. **The winds moving in opposite directions create a tube of rotating air.**

3. **Rising warm air tilts the rotating tube of air from a horizontal to a vertical position.**

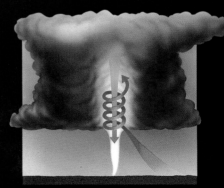

4. **If the rotating tube of air reaches down to the ground, it forms a tornado. Like a giant vacuum cleaner, it sucks up dirt and debris. This gives the tornado its dark color.**

21

Waterspouts

A waterspout is a tornado that forms over a body of water, such as a river, a lake, or an ocean. Waterspouts form in much the same way as tornadoes do. However, instead of picking up dirt from the ground, waterspouts pick up water as they move across it.

Waterspouts are usually smaller, slower, and less damaging than tornadoes. However, they are just as unpredictable. Waterspouts have been known to suck up lizards, tadpoles, frogs, or fish. They have then deposited them on surprised city dwellers miles away! They have also damaged ships. More waterspouts are reported in the lower Florida Keys than anywhere else in the world.

Ships at sea have reported seeing several waterspouts in one day.

Waterspouts can be 20 to 200 feet (6 to 60 meters) in diameter.

In August 2002, severe thunderstorms triggered major flooding in central Europe. Prague, in the Czech Republic, was one of the cities that was badly damaged.

CHAPTER 3

Surviving Storms

A thunderstorm can be thrilling to watch. It can also be extremely dangerous. Lightning, high winds, hail, or floods can injure or even kill people. They can cause millions of dollars' worth of damage to land and property. However, people have survived direct lightning strikes, massive hailstorms, and even tornadoes. Their stories are remarkable.

The 2002 floods were the worst in Prague in 200 years.

Lightning starts about 10,000 forest fires a year in the United States.

Lightning Strikes

Each year in the United States, about 80 people are killed and 300 are injured by lightning. A direct lightning strike is particularly dangerous because the body absorbs all of the electrical charge. Electricity can also jump to a person from a nearby object, such as a tree.

The victim of a lightning strike may suffer serious long-term effects, such as burns, memory loss, and nerve damage. The jolt of electricity can cause the heart or lungs to stop working.

In 2007, Laura Eustermann was in a coma for two weeks after a direct lightning strike. She suffered burns on the top of her head and her legs, where electricity entered and left her body. Eustermann's nerve and muscle pathways were also damaged. She has had to relearn how to move her legs.

A park ranger named Roy Sullivan set the record for surviving lightning strikes. Between 1942 and 1977, he was hit seven times! Lightning knocked Sullivan unconscious, ripped off one of his toenails, set his hair on fire, and blasted him out of his car.

The odds of being struck by lightning in any given year are one in 600,000.

Hailstones can smash windshields and damage roofs. They clog storm drains and kill birds.

Stones and Storms

Hail forms when drops of water in a storm cloud freeze in layers around a bit of ice. Hailstones grow larger as they are tossed about by winds inside the cloud. How large the hailstones become depends on how strong the winds are. When the hailstones in the clouds become too heavy for the winds to carry, they fall to the ground. The largest hailstone ever recovered in the United States was nearly the size of a soccer ball!

On June 22, 2003, a severe thunderstorm pounded Aurora, Nebraska. A giant hailstone smashed into the roof gutter of the Brophy family's house. Thinking fast, the Brophys put the hailstone in the freezer before it could melt. The Brophys' hailstone was one of a kind! It was seven inches (17.8 centimeters) wide.

Winds of more than 90 miles (145 kilometers) per hour create baseball-sized hailstones.

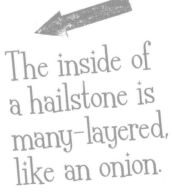

The inside of a hailstone is many-layered, like an onion.

The United States has the most violent tornadoes in the world.

Tornado Damage

Tornadoes are the most violent result of a
thunderstorm. Winds inside a tornado can reach
speeds of 300 miles (480 kilometers) per hour.
The funnel of a tornado is so powerful that it can
pick up livestock, cars, and small buildings.
A tornado damages only things directly in its path.
It may destroy one house and leave the next
house untouched.

Tornado Victims

In April 2002, Emily Ferren of La Plata, Maryland, was driving home. Suddenly, a violent tornado started to sweep up everything around her. Winds of 200 miles (322 kilometers) per hour lifted her car off the ground and deposited it 70 feet (21 meters) away. The car was damaged. Ferren was injured. However, she survived. Five people were killed and 122 others were injured in the same storm. Property damage amounted to $100 million.

This satellite image shows the damage path of the La Plata tornado. The path was nearly 70 miles (113 kilometers) long.

Tornado path

Weather scientists launch weather balloons into thunderstorms to learn more about how tornadoes form.

CHAPTER 4

Weather Watchers

A hundred years ago, people would look at the sky to find out whether a storm was on its way. Today, we tune in to current weather reports on television, the radio, or the Internet. **Meteorologists** gather weather data from more than 10,000 weather stations around the globe. Computers help them put it all together to make forecasts.

 Each day, weather balloons are released at the same time from 900 places around the world.

Storm Warning

If extreme weather is coming, meteorologists send out warnings. A severe thunderstorm *watch* tells you where thunderstorms are likely to occur in the next few hours. A severe thunderstorm *warning* means a storm could be only minutes away. It means that one has been reported by eyewitnesses or detected by weather instruments.

Meteorologists use computers to predict the weather and create weather maps.

Storm Chasers

In order to gather important information about how storms form, some scientists work in teams as "storm chasers." Storm chasers take equipment in cars, trucks, or airplanes to try to get as near as safely possible to storms. They often use special **radar** equipment to measure rain, sleet or snow, wind speed, and wind direction.

Above Earth

Meteorologists rely on a lot of high-tech equipment to know when a storm is coming. For example, each day, they launch hundreds of weather balloons about 15 miles (24 kilometers) into the sky. The helium-filled balloons carry instruments that measure conditions such as air temperature and humidity. The radios attached to the balloons send this information to weather stations on the ground.

The first book on meteorology was written by Aristotle more than 2,300 years ago!

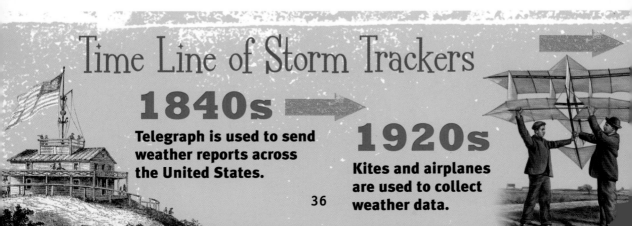

Time Line of Storm Trackers

1840s

Telegraph is used to send weather reports across the United States.

1920s

Kites and airplanes are used to collect weather data.

In Orbit

As high as 22,300 miles (35,900 kilometers) above your head, a fleet of weather satellites orbits

Weather satellite

Earth. The satellites send back all kinds of data about cloud systems, storms, ocean currents, and snow cover, for example. On the ground, **radars** track changes in rainfall and winds. Together, these tools paint a big picture of the weather on its way.

1940s
Radar is used to detect rain and clouds.

1970s
Weather buoys are launched at sea to send weather data to satellites.

In the Philippines, waves lash the shore during tropical thunderstorms.

CHAPTER 5

Run for Cover

Scientists think the number of extreme storms has increased over the past 60 years. For various reasons, they expect this trend to continue. **Global warming** may contribute to an increase in thunderstorms in the future. No matter what the reasons, it is important to know how to stay safe in a thunderstorm.

One thunderstorm can drop as much as 22,000 tons (20,000 metric tons) of rain.

...nd Take Shelter

...to stay safe during a thunderstorm ...well prepared. Listen to weather forecasts. ...a portable radio, a flashlight, and fresh batteries on hand.

If a storm strikes, try to get inside a car or building right away. Once inside, stay away from windows. Don't use the phone or the computer, and unplug appliances. Do not take a bath or shower. Lightning can travel along metal pipes. Wait 30 minutes after the last thunderclap before going outside.

Lightning often strikes the tallest objects in an area. So keep away from trees, power lines, and tall structures.

If you are boating or swimming when a thunderstorm is approaching, return to shore as quickly as possible.

If you take shelter in a car, park away from trees. Don't touch any metal parts inside the car. If you don't make it to shelter, stay away from water or anything metal. If you're in a group, spread out. If you feel your hair stand on end, there is a good chance that lightning is about to strike. Crouch down and make yourself as small a target as possible. Do not lie flat on the ground. Also stay alert for warnings about possible **flash floods**.

Water of Life

For all their fury, thunderstorms are a necessary part of nature. Small fires sparked by lightning can help clear forests for new growth. Thunderstorms also help cool Earth. They carry heat high into space. Thunderstorms carry water, in the form of rain, from oceans and lakes to land. Therefore they are an important part of Earth's water cycle. ★

Storms can damage crops. However, sufficient rain is essential for farms, such as this tea plantation in India.

Energy from one lightning flash: Could power one 100-watt light bulb for 3 months

The odds of being struck by lightning in your lifetime: 1 in 5,000

Time of day that most lightning accidents occur: Between noon and 4:00 p.m.

U.S. city with the most thunderstorm days per year: Tampa, Florida (100)

Falling speed of a baseball-sized hailstone: About 100 mph (160 km/h)

Did you find the truth?

(F) Lightning never strikes the same place twice.

(T) Weather data are gathered from more than 10,000 stations around the world.

Resources

Books

Burby, Liza N. *Electrical Storms*. New York: Rosen Publishing Group, 2005.

Galiano, Dean. *Thunderstorms and Lightning*. New York: Rosen Publishing Group, 2000.

Iwinski, Melissa. *The Wind at Work* (Shockwave Science). New York: Children's Press, 2008.

Netzley, Patricia D. *Thunderstorms*. San Diego: KidHaven Press, 2007.

Scholastic Books. *Our Changing Planet: How Volcanoes, Earthquakes, Tsunamis, and Weather Shape Our Planet* (Scholastic Voyages of Discovery). New York: Scholastic Inc., 1996.

Simon, Seymour. *Lightning*. New York: HarperCollins Children's Books, 2006.

Simon, Seymour. *Tornadoes*. New York: HarperCollins Children's Books, 2001.

World Book Inc. *Thunderstorms*. Chicago: World Book, 2008.

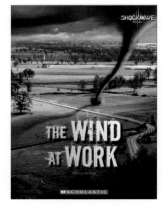

Organizations and Web Sites

National Geographic Kids/Lightning!

www.nationalgeographic.com/ngkids/0406/main.html
Read Sabrina's real-life lightning story and learn
thunderstorm safety tips.

Kidstorm

http://skydiary.com/kids/
Find lots of cool facts about tornadoes, lightning, hurricanes,
and storm chasing. Link up to the latest storm data.

The Weather Channel

www.theweatherchannelkids.com
Get your forecast, play games, and take the Severe Weather
Challenge.

Places to Visit

Museum of Life and Science

433 Murray Avenue
Durham, NC 27704
(919) 220 5429
www.ncmls.org/visit/campus-and-exhibits/exhibits
Walk through a 15-foot-high tornado, play in the clouds, and view satellite imagery.

Museum of Science

Theater of Electricity
Science Park
Boston, MA 02114
(617) 723 2500
http://mos.org/sln/toe/
See a demonstration of a lightning strike and learn about thunderstorm safety.

Important Words

condense – to change from a gas or vapor into a liquid

conductor – something that electricity is able to move through easily

cumulonimbus cloud (kyoom-yuh-loh-NIM-buhss) – a very large, high cloud, with a flat top, that produces thunderstorms

equator – the imaginary line around Earth, halfway between the North Pole and the South Pole

evaporate – to change from a liquid to a gas or vapor

flash flood – sudden flooding caused by heavy rainfall

global warming – a gradual rise in the temperature of Earth's atmosphere

meteorologist – a scientist who studies weather

molecule – the smallest particle into which a substance can be divided while remaining the same substance

radar (RAY-dar) – a device that locates objects by reflecting radio waves off them and receiving the reflected waves

tornado – a whirling, funnel-shaped column of air

tropics – the areas on Earth that lie 1,600 miles (2,575 kilometers) north and south of the equator

Index

Page numbers in **bold** indicate illustrations

About the Author

Chana Stiefel has written several children's books about earthquakes, volcanoes, and other natural disasters. She is a former senior editor of Scholastic's *Science World* magazine. Ms. Stiefel holds a Master's degree in Journalism/Science and Environmental Reporting from New York University. She loves to listen to the sounds of thunderstorms while safe inside her home in Teaneck, New Jersey, with her husband and four children. Another True Book Earth Science title by Ms. Stiefel is *Tsunamis*.